Cool Caves

THIS EDITION
Editorial Management by Oriel Square
Produced for DK by WonderLab Group LLC
Jennifer Emmett, Erica Green, Kate Hale, *Founders*

Editors Grace Hill Smith, Libby Romero, Maya Myers, Michaela Weglinski;
Photography Editors Kelley Miller, Annette Kiesow, Nicole di Mella; **Managing Editor** Rachel Houghton;
Designers Project Design Company; **Researcher** Michelle Harris; **Copy Editor** Lori Merritt;
Indexer Connie Binder; **Proofreader** Larry Shea; **Reading Specialist** Dr. Jennifer Albro;
Curriculum Specialist Elaine Larson

Published in the United States by DK Publishing
1745 Broadway, 20th Floor, New York, NY 10019

Copyright © 2023 Dorling Kindersley Limited
DK, a Division of Penguin Random House LLC
24 25 26 10 9 8 7 6 5 4 3
003-334013-Oct/2023

All rights reserved.

Without limiting the rights under the copyright reserved above, no part of this publication may be reproduced, stored in or introduced into a retrieval system, or transmitted, in any form, or by any means (electronic, mechanical, photocopying, recording, or otherwise), without the prior written permission of the copyright owner.
Published in Great Britain by Dorling Kindersley Limited

A catalog record for this book
is available from the Library of Congress.
HC ISBN: 978-0-7440-7362-1
PB ISBN: 978-0-7440-7363-8

DK books are available at special discounts when purchased in bulk for sales promotions, premiums, fundraising, or educational use. For details, contact: DK Publishing Special Markets,
1745 Broadway, 20th Floor, New York, NY 10019
SpecialSales@dk.com

Printed and bound in China

The publisher would like to thank the following for their kind permission to reproduce their images:
a=above; c=center; b=below; l=left; r=right; t=top; b/g=background

Alamy Stock Photo: agefotostock / Sami Sarkis 23b, Natalia Pryanishnikova 12-13b, Westend61 GmbH / Martin Siepmann 14, Rudmer Zwerver 27br; **Dreamstime.com:** Aiisha 17, Dslaven 19cra, Sandra Foyt 11br, Kateryna Kon 25br, Julia Kuznetsova 1cb, Olena Lysytsia 20crb, Manon14 18-19t, Suse Schulz 13crb, Sjors737 9br; **Getty Images:** 500px / Christopher Cullen 20br, Corbis Documentary / Douglas Peebles 22b, Photodisc / Nancy Nehring 11t; **Getty Images / iStock:** MarcelStrelow 26t, milehightraveler 6-7; **NASA:** JPL 23tl; **Science Photo Library:** Javier Trueba / MSF 3cb, 24t; **Shutterstock.com:** Aerial-motion 28-29, Altosvic 21, Ales Cesen 16br, kid315 8t, ouran 8tl (pointer), 10tr (pointer), 13tr (pointer), 15tr (pointer), 17tl (pointer), 18tl (pointer), 21tr (pointer), 22tr (pointer), 24tl (pointer), 27tr (pointer), Soloma 8tl (Globe), 10tr (Globe), 13tr (Globe), 15tr (Globe), 17tl (Globe), 18tl (Globe), 21tr (Globe), 22tr (Globe), 24tl (Globe), 27tr (Globe), Vladimir Shutter 15bl, Sigit Adhi Wibowo 4-5

Cover images: *Front:* **Dreamstime.com:** Rixie

All other images © Dorling Kindersley
For more information see: www.dkimages.com

For the curious
www.dk.com

Level 3

Cool Caves

Libby Romero

Contents

6	Discovering Caves
8	Son Doong Cave
10	Mammoth Cave
12	Sac Actun Cave System
15	Eisriesenwelt Cave
16	Crystal Cave
18	Marble Caves

20	Fingal's Cave
22	Kazumura Cave
24	Cave of Crystals
26	Waitomo Caves
30	Glossary
31	Index
32	Quiz

Discovering Caves

Come on in! It's dark. It's chilly. And it's very quiet inside a cave. It's so quiet that you can hear bats flying, insects crawling, and water dripping down from the surface above. Sounds bounce off the walls and echo throughout the hollow chamber. The total darkness makes them seem louder than they really are.

Carlsbad Caverns
New Mexico, USA

Caves are a part of nature. They can be found underground, in hillsides, or on the sides of cliffs. There are caves inside glaciers and hardened lava, too. Caves can be pretty cool!

Some caves are smaller than a classroom. Others are so big that entire city blocks could fit inside them. Many caves have an opening large enough for a person to pass through. And every cave has a chamber that goes back farther than sunlight can filter in. Within that dark space lies a world of creatures and features just waiting to be explored.

Son Doong Cave

Son Doong Cave in Vietnam is the world's largest cave. It wasn't discovered until 1990. A local man found it after he saw clouds billowing from its opening. When he got closer, he heard the sounds of a raging river coming from inside. He couldn't wait to show someone the cave he had found.

Unfortunately, the cave is hidden in the middle of a jungle, and it took the man 18 years to find that opening again! When he did, he guided explorers to the cave.

Inside, two rivers join together and flow along a fault line—a large crack in Earth's surface. That's why the cave's passages are so huge.

Deep in the cave, the explorers found rainforests growing from the cave's floor. The cave ceiling had collapsed to create two giant openings. Sunlight shines through the openings to the plants and trees below.

Mighty Large

Son Doong Cave, which means "mountain river cave," formed about three million years ago. The main cavern is so big that an entire city block of 40-story skyscrapers could fit inside its chamber.

Mammoth Cave

Mammoth Cave is the world's longest cave system. It lies beneath the woodlands of central Kentucky in the United States. The cave started to form 10 to 15 million years ago. Rainwater seeped through cracks in limestone rock. It combined with carbon dioxide to create a weak acid. The acid dissolved the rocks. This is how most caves form. They are called solution caves.

Flowing water created five levels of passageways inside Mammoth Cave. Dripping water combined with minerals to create lots of different cave formations, such as stalactites and stalagmites.

The northern cavefish lives inside Mammoth Cave. The fish is white and has no eyes. It has adapted over time to live in total darkness.

Stalactites hang down from the ceiling. Stalagmites rise up from the floor. Sheets of minerals form curtain-shaped deposits called flowstone along the cave's walls. Little knobs called cave popcorn grow in the cave, too. Can you guess how they got their name?

Carlsbad Caverns
Carlsbad Caverns in New Mexico, USA, are solution caves, too. But these caves formed in a different way. Gases from oil deposits in the ground and tiny microbes combined with oxygen in the air, creating an acid that dissolved the rocks.

Sac Actun Cave System

The second-longest cave system in the world is Sac Actun. It lies along the Caribbean coast in Mexico's Yucatán Peninsula. It's a bit harder to explore these passageways—they're underwater! To enter, divers plunge into a deep sinkhole called a cenote. There are more than 220 cenotes within the Sac Actun system.

Sac Actun's passageways weren't always underwater. Deep inside, divers have found hidden treasures that reveal clues about the past. There are ceramics, drawings on cave walls, and even a shrine to the Mayan god of war and commerce. Divers have also found the remains of ancient humans. There are bones of animals, like saber-toothed tigers, too.

Ancient Mayans considered caves to be sacred places—especially the Sac Actun caves that led to water.

Lascaux Cave

Another cave that has taught us about the past is the Lascaux Cave in France. Around 600 paintings, mostly of animals, and 1,400 engravings decorate the cave's walls. The artwork was created around 17,000 to 15,000 BCE.

Eisriesenwelt Cave

Frozen water, or ice, is what makes the Eisriesenwelt Cave in the Austrian Alps so spectacular. It is an ice cave. An ice cave is a cave formed in stone that has ice in it all year long.

Because of how air moves through the lower parts of this cave, the temperature is always freezing there. As water drips in, it freezes to create fantastic ice sculptures. Eisriesenwelt is the largest ice cave in the world. Some of the ice in it is about 1,000 years old.

Giant Ice

Eisriesenwelt is a German word. It means "world of ice giants." Inside the cave, there are stalactites, stalagmites, domes, and even waterfalls made out of ice.

Crystal Cave

Glacier caves are often mistakenly called ice caves. But these caves actually form inside glaciers. There are lots of glacier caves in Iceland. Crystal Cave in the Vatnajökull Glacier is one of the most famous. It is on Iceland's coast.

Ice on the walls and ceiling of this cave is a beautiful aquamarine blue. The ice on its floor is nearly black. The walls are smooth, especially the farther in you go. And the passages are narrow. That makes it easy to hear the glacier pop and crackle as it moves.

Safety First
During summer, glacier caves melt. Often, they collapse. That's why these caves can only be explored during winter, when the ice is frozen and the caves are stable. It's also why you should only enter these caves with an experienced guide.

Marble Caves

The Marble Caves, rising along General Carrera Lake in Chile, are some of the most beautiful caves in the world. Over the past 6,000 years, waves pounding the pure marble cliffs have sculpted the caves. The caves have smooth, curved walls. They are lined with swirling patterns of blue.

Sea Caves
Although they're on a lake, the Marble Caves are sea caves. Sea caves form in cliffs that line an ocean or lake. Waves break down the rock as they smash into the coast.

The blue color is a reflection. It comes from glacial water in the lake. The shade of blue changes depending on the lake's water level and the time of year. In spring, when water levels are lower, the walls are bright turquoise. In summer, when the water is deeper, the walls are a dark navy blue.

Fingal's Cave

The walls of Fingal's Cave on Scotland's Staffa Island are lined with massive six-sided columns of basalt. Basalt is a type of volcanic rock. According to legend, the cave is the work of a giant. It is one end of a bridge that the giant built so he could cross from Ireland to Scotland to fight another giant.

In reality, the rocky columns were formed by lava that flowed and cooled about 60 million years ago. Ocean waves, chipping away at the rocks, created the cave over time.

Pleasant Tune

Fingal's Cave is also known for its music. The sound of the waves bounces off the cave's arched roof. This produces a beautiful melody.

Kazumura Cave

Around 500 years ago, the Kīlauea volcano on the Big Island of Hawai'i erupted. Lava flowed down the volcano's sides. The lava on top cooled, grew thicker, and moved more slowly. Eventually, it hardened into a thick crust.

Hotter, faster lava flowed like a river beneath the crust. It formed a tube as the lava kept flowing underneath the cooled top. When the eruption stopped, the lava drained out of the tube.

hot lava flowing inside a lava tube

Lunar Lava Tubes
Scientists think there are lava tubes on the Moon, too. If so, they may be good places to build lunar bases. An underground base would protect astronauts from meteoroid strikes and huge changes in temperature.

As the tube cooled, a tunnel formed inside. It stretches for more than 40 miles (64 km). This is the Kazumura Cave, which is thought to be the longest lava tube in the world.

Cave of Crystals

In the year 2000, miners in Mexico discovered the Cave of Crystals. It is one of the most unusual caves on Earth. Shaped like a horseshoe, the cave is filled with giant crystals. Some of the crystals are more than 36 feet (11 m) tall and 3.2 feet (1 m) thick.

Scientists believe that groundwater flooded the cave about 500,000 years ago. A pool of magma heated it from below. The hot water came in contact with cool water from above, and crystals began to grow. The water's temperature held steady, so the crystals kept growing.

Though the cave is beautiful, it is dangerous. When researchers explore inside, they can only stay for a short time. Temperatures in the cave can rise up to 136°F (58°C). And the relative humidity stays around 100 percent. The heat and the humidity can be deadly, as the moisture in the air can condense in a person's lungs.

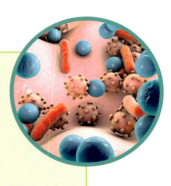

Tiny Life
Scientists found tiny microbes in the Cave of Crystals that have been dormant for up to 50,000 years! There is nothing else like them on Earth.

Waitomo Caves

Long ago, powerful underground streams cut through layers of limestone in New Zealand. This created the Waitomo cave system. The caves are cool, but it's what lives inside that sparks people's imaginations—literally!

The Waitomo Caves are filled with glowworms. These larvae of a species of gnat look like maggots. Their tails are bioluminescent. They contain chemicals that react with oxygen to produce an eerie blue light.

That blue glow is beautiful to humans. But it has a deadly purpose. It attracts other insects. The glowworms spin a sticky thread that hangs down from the cave roof. When prey approaches the light, it gets stuck in the thread. Just like a spider's web, the glowworm's thread captures a meal.

Cave Crickets

Glowworms get all the attention, but other animals live in the Waitomo Caves, too—including the Waitomo cave weta. These big cave crickets have been around since the days of the dinosaurs. They gather near cave openings during the day and come out at night to eat.

No matter how a cave was formed or what you can find inside, caves are fascinating places to explore. They may be dark. They may be damp. They may hold creatures you've never seen before.

Some caves have been around for thousands or even millions of years. They hold secrets to Earth's past. They reveal clues about how people once lived. They show how animals evolved over time. Caves are pretty cool. Wouldn't you agree?

Glossary

Bioluminescent
[by-oh-loo-min-ESS-ent]
Able to give off light as a living
organism, such as a firefly

Cave
A natural underground chamber
that has an opening to the surface

Cenote
[si-NO-tay]
A deep sinkhole filled with water

Chamber
A large room

Crystal
A substance that forms a pattern of
many flat surfaces when it becomes
a solid

Fault line
A large crack in Earth's surface

Flowstone
Minerals deposited by a thin sheet
of water along the walls or floor of
a cave

Glacier
A large mass of slowly moving ice

Glowworm
A worm-shaped insect that can
produce and give off light from
its body

Hollow
Having an unfilled space inside

Lava
Hot, molten rock that comes out of
an erupting volcano and hardens
as it cools

Magma
Molten rock found beneath Earth's
surface that forms lava when it
flows out of volcanoes

Stalactite
[stuh-LACK-tite]
A deposit of minerals that hangs
down from the roof or sides of
a cave

Stalagmite
[stuh-LAG-mite]
A deposit of minerals that builds
up from a cave floor

Index

basalt 20

bioluminescent 27

Carlsbad Caverns, New Mexico, USA 6, 11

cave crickets 27

Cave of Crystals, Mexico 24–25

cenotes 12

chamber 6, 7, 9

crickets 27

Crystal Cave, Iceland 16–17

crystals 24–25

Eisriesenwelt Cave, Austria 14–15

fault line 9

Fingal's Cave, Scotland 20–21

fish 10

flowstone 11

glacier caves 16–17

glowworms 27

ice caves 14–15, 16

Kazumura Cave, Hawai'i, USA 22–23

Lascaux Cave, France 13

lava 20, 22–23

magma 25

Mammoth Cave, Kentucky, USA 10–11

Marble Caves, Chile 18–19

microbes 25

music 20

northern cavefish 10

Sac Actun Cave System, Mexico 12–13

safety 16, 25

sea caves 19

size of caves 7, 9

solution caves 10, 11

Son Doong Cave, Vietnam 8–9

sounds 6, 20

stalactites 10–11, 15

stalagmites 10–11, 15

underwater caves 12–13, 18–19

volcanoes 22

Waitomo Caves, New Zealand 26–27

weta 27

Quiz

Answer the questions to see what you have learned. Check your answers in the key below.

1. Where is the world's largest cave?
2. What is the most common type of cave on Earth?
3. What is the difference between a stalactite and a stalagmite?
4. Why is it difficult to explore the Sac Actun cave system?
5. What kind of cave is the Eisriesenwelt Cave in the Austrian Alps?
6. What do the Marble Caves in Chile and Fingal's Cave in Scotland have in common?
7. What did miners discover in a cave in Mexico?
8. What are the Waitomo Caves in New Zealand known for?

1. Vietnam 2. A solution cave 3. Stalactites hang down from a cave ceiling and stalagmites rise up from the floor 4. It is underwater 5. An ice cave 6. Both were formed by waves 7. Giant crystals 8. Glowworms